Notes of a Seer

Ian Ormesher

2019

Cover Design by Freepik. Artwork by Anna Goodman.

First Printing: 2019

ISBN 978-0-244-90271-1

Dedication

To Mandy.

You're amazing and I'm so grateful to God for Him bringing you into my life. I love you deeply. You're the wisest person I know. You gave me such unconditional love when I first met you. God put the pieces of my heart back together through you. We've been on such an adventure together over the years. I know our adventures haven't stopped yet and I'm looking forward to what God has in store for us.

Yureverluvinhubby,

Ian

P.S. I know you don't read books but I was hoping this dedication might tempt you to read this one ☺

Contents

Endorsements

"Ian invites us into the world of prophetic revelation with grace, clarity and humility. Jesus is still speaking today and this book will encourage you to keep listening and keep looking for what He is doing in the earth today. Read and enjoy!" - **Phil Wilthew**, senior leader at Kings Arms Church, Bedford and author of two books, 'Developing Prophetic Culture' and 'Multiplying Disciples'.

"I always look forward to reading/hearing what Ian has to say, and he hasn't disappointed me yet. This book is full of practical help, taking away the 'mystery' of being a seer and making the steps accessible to all. I appreciate his knowledge of the bible and how he remains biblical and undergirds what he says, with Scripture. This is the only way to do it and he does it well. I trust that as you read, you will be stirred, encouraged and motivated to step out in these things yourself. It is the inheritance of the children of God and Ian displays it well. Enjoy reading and let's get the Army of God, the Church, motivated, equipped and stirred for the nations and God's Glory in them. The time is now." **- Angela Kemm**, Prophetic Evangelist, City Church Cambridge

"Accessible, Faith stirring, Encouraging, Provoking.... Ian's second book builds on his first 'Journey of a Seer'. His heart for making the prophetic accessible for all means the book is full of helpful explanations and illustrations from his own life. Ian practices what he teaches and provokes our prophetic journey! His book will equip and would form the basis of a great curriculum for a prophetic team to work through." – **Adrian Horner**, senior leader of Open Door Church, Kettering.

Acknowledgements

First I would like to say thank you to Jesus, who took all my sin on the cross and gave me new life. He turned my life around.

I'd also like to thank Karina Pahls. She led me to the Lord when she was a German exchange student in Liverpool. I've never seen her since and would love to tell her I'm still following Jesus after all these years. She was brave enough to tell a scary man about Jesus when others wouldn't dare. I am truly eternally grateful.

I'd like to thank Angela Kemm. She continues to challenge and stretch me and I am so grateful for all the time she gives me. She knows where my limits are and will always push me one step beyond. That's where I like to be, because that's where I find God.

I'd like to thank Anna Goodman, who helped me once again with this new book. Her comments and advice have been invaluable and encouraging. I've enjoyed watching her grow and flourish in the prophetic over the years. Long may that continue!

Introduction

After I wrote my first book, 'Journey of a Seer', I found people would have lots of questions when they met me. They enjoyed my story, but it raised a number of things for them that they wanted to know more about. That was when I decided to write a second book to answer those questions that they raised and also, hopefully, others that hadn't yet been asked. I've obviously looked deeply into the Word of God to try and find answers for my own questions about the experiences that I was having. I discovered that others in the Bible had similar experiences too and they were really helpful in trying to unpack things. This book is about the things I found.

I am sure that there will still be some people who have even more questions to ask! I hope I'll have the opportunity to meet you some time and we can sit down and chat about them over a coffee. The Christian life is exciting and powerful. It was never meant to be dull. I hope this book spurs you on towards love and good deeds.

Chapter 1: Ministering from the Front

When I was living in Hong Kong I went to a small China conference where Jackie Pullinger was speaking. She's an amazing lady who left the UK to go to Hong Kong with just her clarinet and a call from God and ended up doing an amazing work amongst drug addicts. She planted a church which is still growing and thriving to this day. She did a seminar in the afternoon with some members of her Church who had come along to help her. There weren't many people in the room and she invited the Holy Spirit to come and minister to people. I found myself standing near her. She turned to one of her team members and said, pointing to someone who was standing nearby with their eyes closed and hands help up, "Look at that lady there. See how the Holy Spirit is all over her! Go over and minster to her." I looked at the lady and I can only say that I clearly saw the Holy Spirit all over her. I know Jackie was talking to her team member, but I learnt an important lesson that day. I learnt what the Holy Spirit looks like when He's ministering to people. Since that time I've been able to see the same thing over people when the Holy Spirit is ministering to them too. A second really important thing I've learnt since is that just because the Holy Spirit is ministering to someone it doesn't mean we have permission to minister too. We should always co-operate with what He is doing. Ask Him what to do. Sometimes He will tell us to hold back and let Him continue to do His work. Always follow His lead. If He tells us to hold back, simply pray in tongues over the person and see what happens.

I've watched people prophesy from the front of a meeting and wondered how they knew who they should call out. So a few years ago I decided that I would be brave and simply ask them!

Notes of a Seer

One person I asked said they would simply see the person glow. It was like God was pointing the person out. Because they had prophesied over several people, I asked them how they knew what order to prophesy. They said they would do them in the same order that they were pointed out.

I asked Angela Kemm the same question and she said that God would "highlight" the person before the meeting began. She would stand around looking out over the congregation, looking for the people that God was "highlighting". She then knew those were the people she would minister to later on. I then asked her what she meant by "highlight". For her, there was something about them that seemed to be catching her attention. It was like God was drawing them to her. He was "highlighting" them.

For Shawn Bolz and Julian Adams who are both amazing prophets, God gives them a word of knowledge that they will then call out, waiting for someone to respond. The person who responds is the one they will prophesy over, using the word of knowledge they got. That's quite straightforward – if you can get the word of knowledge to start with!

For James Maloney, again another amazing prophet, he will see a shaft of light that then points to the person. Or he will call out a word of knowledge, like Shawn and Julian.

For me, I've been on a bit of a journey. It started with seeing in the Spirit objects in boxes on the stage. I would then look out at the congregation and seeing each of the objects over specific people. That was during worship. I then knew the people I should prophesy over, and the object was my word of knowledge for them. I would then ask God what each of the objects meant and that would be the starting point for my prophesying over the person. So when this first started happening it was during the worship time at a meeting.

Then, for a while, I would do what Angela did. I would look around at the start of the meeting, looking for the objects over different people. This was even before the worship time. Then when it came time to minister from the front, I would look for the people again to see their object, ask God what it meant and then prophesy from that.

God grows and stretches us step-by-step. I found that once I understood how God was showing me things and became comfortable with that, He decided to stretch me further! I'm always praying that He will stretch me more so that I can grow in faith and He takes my requests seriously! Now I don't have anything before I start to prophesy from the front. I'll start by saying, "I'm now going to give out a few words" even though at that point I don't have anything. But I've committed myself in faith, and start looking around. If there's lots of people in the meeting and I can't clearly see the back row, I'll walk out amongst the people, looking for the objects to appear above their heads. If nothing appears, at least I get some exercise.

Accountability

One of the benefits of prophesying from the front is that it gives you accountability. It means other people can judge the word you give. It is also a way of honouring the person publicly.

Notes of a Seer

Chapter 2: Words of Knowledge

> Now concerning spiritual gifts, brethren, I do not want you to be ignorant … But the manifestation of the Spirit is given to each one for the profit of all: for to one is given the word of wisdom through the Spirit, to another the word of knowledge through the same Spirit, (1Co 12:1 NKJV)

In 1 Corinthians 12 Paul talks about the gifts of the Spirit. Amongst the nine gifts listed there we find one we call "word of knowledge".

Before I go on and talk about words of knowledge, it's worth noting that there are 4 things Paul tells us in his letters that he does not want Christians to be ignorant of.:

These are:

• Gifts of the Spirit (1 Co 12:1)

• God's future plan for the Jews after the full number of the Gentiles have been saved (Rom 11:25)

• What happens to Christians after they die (1 Thess 4:13)

• Satan's schemes (2 Co 2:11)

Even though Paul tells us not to be ignorant about these things, I'm sure most of you won't have heard teaching about the latter two. Please can I encourage you not to be an ignorant Christian - read what Paul says about these four things. They were written to encourage you and give you hope.

Notes of a Seer

Back to words of knowledge. Paul elaborates on them in another passage:

> Now we have received, not the spirit of the world, but the Spirit who is from God, that we might know the things that have been freely given to us by God. These things we also speak, not in words which man's wisdom teaches but which the Holy Spirit teaches (1 Co 2:12-13 NKJV)

This gives us the definition for a word of knowledge:

A **word of knowledge** is a supernatural revelation of information received through the Holy Spirit.

It's important to note the supernatural part of this. It isn't knowledge that has been received by human or natural means.

Words of knowledge can be used with the prophetic and with healing. People like Shawn Bolz and Julian Adams are really good examples of using words of knowledge in the prophetic. The Holy Spirit gives them words of knowledge to identify people that they will then prophesy over. And as they're prophesying He will often give them more words.

Words of knowledge are like Jesus calling out to you – in the same way that He called out to Blind Bartimaeus. We read about it in Mark 10. The people said to Bartimaeus, "He's calling you":

> Then they came to Jericho. As Jesus and his disciples, together with a large crowd, were leaving the city, a blind man, Bartimaeus (that is, the Son of Timaeus), was sitting by the roadside begging. When he heard that it was Jesus of Nazareth, he began to shout, "Jesus, Son of David, have mercy on me!" Many rebuked him and told him to be quiet, but he

shouted all the more, "Son of David, have mercy on me!" Jesus stopped and said, "Call him." So they called to the blind man, "Cheer up! On your feet! He's calling you." Throwing his cloak aside, he jumped to his feet and came to Jesus. "What do you want me to do for you?" Jesus asked him. The blind man said, "Rabbi, I want to see." "Go," said Jesus, "your faith has healed you." Immediately he received his sight and followed Jesus along the road. (Mar 10:1 NIV)

That's exactly what a word of knowledge is. It's Jesus calling the person.

7 Ways that Words of Knowledge come – The Dress Fits

There are seven different ways that words of knowledge can come. To help you remember them, I've created an acronym:

The DRESS FiTs

<u>Dream it</u>

I had a dream once, and in that dream I was in a healing meeting and Randy Clark was giving out words of knowledge. He said there was someone there with the name Martina, that she had a pain in her shoulder and a pain in her hip. When I woke up I thought, "That is a word of knowledge!" I wrote it down and then gave it that evening as a word of knowledge. Sure enough, a lady called Martina came up for prayer. She said she had a pain in her shoulder and a pain in her hip that she had had since giving birth. I prayed for her and all the pain went away! She was healed.

I had another dream where I was sitting at a desk with a blank piece of paper in front of me. I then wrote down the first line of a prophetic word. When I woke up, I immediately wrote down that first line that I'd seen in the dream. Then God gave me the rest of the word, and also told me who the word was for.

God can give words of knowledge in dreams. Ask Him to speak to you in your dreams, just before you go to sleep. I do that every night. Keep a notebook by the side of your bed so you can write down anything He says.

Read it

You may see (with spiritual sight) a word written across the front or back of a person. You might see the word written above them or on a wall by them or on the floor near them. You see this as writing that you can actually read. I've seen angels holding up pieces of card with words written on them. Read it and give it as a word of knowledge.

Experience it

This is very similar to dreaming it, but you're actually awake and it's a vivid vision. The experience is so strong that it feels as if you're part of it, rather than just observing it.

See it

This is one of the main ways that God speaks to me with words of knowledge. You can see an object that is actually a word of knowledge for that person.

Say it

Whilst praying or talking with someone you may find yourself saying things you hadn't thought about. They simply come out spontaneously, but you know that it's from God.

<u>Feel it</u>

This is the most common form of words of knowledge for healing, but it can also be used in the prophetic.

<u>Think it</u>

You may sense in your mind that someone has a particular problem or issue. It comes as an impression that you feel is from the Lord.

<u>Smell it</u>

I was in a meeting once and I began to smell fire. I started to get concerned because I thought that maybe there was a real fire. Just then the speaker said, "Some of you are smelling fire. That's because there's a revival coming and God wants to use you in it!"

Another time I was in a meeting sitting next to a secret smoker. He'd pop out during the breaks and come back smelling of smoke. One time after he came back I began to smell apples. It was a really strong smell and I realised it wasn't anyone around me because all I could smell was smoke! Then the speaker announced that he could smell apples and this was because God wanted to bring freedom to some people who were there. He mentioned some specific things and each time got people to stand and be prayed for.

Then I was in a meeting and had a strong smell of incense – like someone had lit a josh stick. Again the person leading the meeting said that he could smell incense and this represented the prayers of the saints so we were to spend some time in prayer.

I'm slowly building up a dictionary of smells and what they signify!

Words of Knowledge – Birthday Months

A good way of stepping out in words of knowledge is to ask God to give you a word of knowledge for someone's birthday month. If you were to simply guess, then you've got a 1 in 12 chance of getting it right. But if God is giving it to you, it will be a lot more accurate. God speaks to us in different ways so it's important to try and work out how He wants to speak to you. There's a process in this. I'll show you how it worked for me, but don't think this is the only way that God can do it. You need to co-operate with Him and try different things. Since I think in numbers (for my work) I had a go at assigning a different object to each month. Then when I saw the object, I'd know it was for that month. I went through my contacts, asking God to show me who He wanted to speak to. Then I asked Him to show me their birthday month with a picture. I would then contact that person asking them if that month was their birthday month. If I got it right, then it would be confirmation for me that God wanted me to give that person a prophetic word. I would then ask God for a word and share it with the person. I also made a note of how I'd got the month so I could see what was working and what wasn't. After a while I was getting about 1 in 3 months right. So I thought it was time to crank it up and take more risk!

Words of Knowledge – Significant Dates

Significant dates are in a different league. If you were simply guessing, you've got a 1 in 365 chance of getting it right. So how will you get them? Again, there's a process and you need to discover what works for you. Shawn Bolz gets them as Bible verses. He'll get something like "Hebrews 11:4". Because American dates have month then day, this would be equivalent to November-4, that is to say 4th November. If you are British this would be April-11, which is quite a different date. I tried this at first, but the only Bible verses I got were the Bible verses I knew, which wasn't very helpful!

Chapter 2: Words of Knowledge

For me, I already had a way God could show me the month, so I just needed a way for God to show me the day. But now it was getting complicated!

What I've found is that you often just need to step out in faith and do it. Learn from your mistakes. Always be gracious and loving to the person. When you get it wrong I've found it useful to say something like this, "I'm just trying to ask God for Words of Knowledge and I clearly need to listen better". I've found most people are very gracious. Some are very encouraging. If you don't step out and take risks you'll never grow in faith or get any right.

I keep a record of who I've given a word of knowledge to, how it came (Dress Fits) and whether it was right or wrong. There's a process in this, and I'm trying to learn how God speaks to me and reveals these things to me.

Let me give you an example of a significant date I got for someone, how it came, and what the outcome was.

I was at a conference and I had a dream. In this dream I saw a lady I'd met there, who I knew was married. She was holding a ticket. This ticket was a family ticket for an event. It was for 2 adults and 2 children. The ticket had a date on it, which was the date of the event. It was 28th March. When I woke up I asked the Lord about it and what it meant. The date, the 28th March, is actually the day I became a Christian. God said this ticket was a promise to the lady for her two children, that they would become Christians and stay Christians.

At this point I didn't know if the lady had any children. I only knew she was married. And if she did have children, I also didn't know how many. Sometime during the conference that day there was a ministry time. I went up to the lady and said I had a word for her. I asked her if she had any children. She said she did. Two. I asked her if they were Christians or not and she said she wasn't sure. Now I'm thinking this all fits and I can tell her what God showed me and told me. But I thought I'd first ask her if the 28th March was a significant date for her. This is where it started to get weird! She said it was. It was her Dad's birthday. When she said this I started to well up, because that date is not just the day when I became a Christian but it was also my Dad's birthday! So I asked her if her Dad was a Christian and she said no. Finally I was able to share what I had dreamed and what God had said. I also said that the promise of salvation wasn't just for her kids but also for her Dad.

Words of Knowledge – Names

Shawn Bolz is really good at getting these. Sometimes he will see the face of another person that he knows superimposed on the face of the person in front of him. He then knows that the name of the person in front of him is the name of the superimposed person. Sometimes he'll have a song run through his head and the name of the artist who sings it is the name of the person in front of him.

When someone's name is given, it can be very encouraging for them and builds faith. God knows their name.

The only names I've got so far have been in dreams. God has also given me names of people's angels. That's a difficult one to verify, though, because they obviously don't appear with nametags that everyone can see! Having said that, sometimes when I've given a name the person will "know" that the name is right. There's a confirmation in their spirit. Other times the meaning of the name is something significant for them.

Words of Knowledge – Numbers

Numbers can be great for words of knowledge. 4-digit numbers can be passcodes for phones, bank account PINs. 6-digit numbers can be the same. 6-digit numbers can also be dates of birth. 8-digit numbers can be bank account numbers. I've seen both Shawn Bolz and Julian Adams give these out and people respond.

I was due to preach and minister at a Church one time and the night before I had a dream. In the dream I looked and a mobile phone number appeared. I read out the phone number and someone responded. I then prophesied over them. When I woke up I felt this was an encouragement from the Lord to step out and have a go at doing this at the Church I was going to.

In the car on the way down I realised I had no idea how many digits there were in a mobile phone number. So I thought I would go for a part of the number. 4-digits you could guess, but 6-digits would work. I told the Lord I had faith for 6-digits of a phone number and please could he show me that, rather than all the numbers I'd seen in the dream.

After I'd finished preaching I started to give out some words, prophesying over the objects I was seeing over people. Once I'd done that I knew I needed to step out with the 6-digits. Because I'd never done this before, I had no idea where the digits would appear. Would they be over someone's head? Would they be in the air? I began to look around to see if I could see them. There was no numbers over any one. No numbers in the air over everyone. Then I looked over to my right, where there was a white wall. As I was looking at this, 6-digits appeared. I'd found them! I read them out, one by one, and asked if they meant anything to anyone. No-one replied, so I said that if maybe they had meant something to someone but they were too embarrassed to own up publicly, I'd be happy to chat with them after the meeting and share the word with them.

After the meeting I was having a drink and a lady came up to me. She said it was such a shame, but those 6 digits had almost been the last 6 digits of her mobile phone number. There was just one digit wrong. At that point I felt a gentle rebuke from the Lord. If I'd trusted the dream and what He'd originally shown me and not tried to reduce the number of digits to something I felt was more viable, He would have given me the whole thing. Next time I'll be more obedient.

Words of Knowledge – Addresses

I've seen Shawn Bolz and others call out an address that was significant for someone. The fact that God knows where a person lives can be very encouraging for them. A friend of mine gave out an address one time and it turned out to be the new address for someone. They were just in the process of moving house and the fact that God knew their new address was encouraging for them and helped them to see that God was in the move and they could trust Him.

Words of Knowledge – Others

I've included some of the most common things that can be revealed with words of knowledge. But there are a lot more things that He can reveal. Things like:

- Job

- Marital status

- Children

- Siblings

- Hobbies

For me, the object that I see over someone can often be a word of knowledge itself. An example of this was when I once saw a pair of dancing shoes over someone and gave them a word about them dancing before the Lord and His delight as they did this. I found out later that she was actually a professional dancer and the word was very encouraging for her.

Words of Knowledge – Don't Cheat!

Never be tempted to cheat with words of knowledge - to present information you know in the natural as something that God has revealed to you supernaturally. If you know someone's birthday or some significant fact about them, don't give it to them and pretend you don't know it already. It's cheating. It's deceptive. That isn't how God works. If you're not sure about whether a fact you're about to reveal is something you would already know about them then ask them. Ask them if you would have known that naturally about them. It's better to be safe. It honours the Lord and it keeps you accountable.

Whenever I go to a Church I make it a point to stay away from any notice boards or other sources of Church information. If they've got a magazine I won't read it. I'll be very careful about visiting their website, if they have one. I will avoid their "vision" page or "meet the team". I won't look them up on Facebook either. All of that is before I minister. Afterwards I can look at all of that.

The thing about all of this is that you could do it. You could find out information online or elsewhere and you could then give it as a word of knowledge. People would think it was God. But you would know it wasn't. Then you'd have to keep doing that. To keep lying. It's an awful spiral to get into. What you build in the flesh would have to be maintained in the flesh. Don't do it!

Words of Knowledge to pass an exam

I thought that title might get your attention! I became a Christian just before my second year exams at university. I hadn't been a good student. I'd skived a lot of the lectures and so was missing a lot of notes for my subjects. Now I had become a Christian I wanted to do well, but I was missing a lot of stuff. So when I went to take my exams I prayed desperately to God. I asked Him to show me which questions I should answer and also could He please give me words of knowledge so I could actually answer the questions! And that's exactly what God did. I managed to scrape through all my exams even though I didn't deserve to. That was the grace of God. I tell my kids that this can't be their strategy for exams. They need to study properly. My case was special circumstances!

Because I'd scraped through my exams the university told me I couldn't take an honours degree but only a basic degree. I appealed against this and in my appeal hearing I told them how Jesus had just recently saved me and turned my life around. Now I was a different person and I believed I could do the honours course and pass, with Jesus' help and hard work. I was allowed to do it, but they were very clear that if I failed I couldn't resit and would end up with nothing. I did pass my last year and did really well, but because the low marks from my second year were also taken into account I ended up with a 2-2 honours degree. Living in Cambridge that is looked down upon and there are quite a few employers who won't even consider me for a job because of it. But for me, it's a testament of the grace of God and how He changed me and gave me a new life. To Him be the glory!

Chapter 3: Knowing Hearts

> Now some teachers of the law were sitting there, thinking to themselves, "Why does this fellow talk like that? He's blaspheming! Who can forgive sins but God alone?" Immediately Jesus knew in his spirit that this was what they were thinking in their hearts, and he said to them, "Why are you thinking these things? (Mar 2:6-8 NIV)

These verses are part of an incident that Mark recorded about the time when a paralytic was lowered through the roof by his friends and Jesus healed him of his paralysis and forgave his sins at the same time. I'm sure you've read it many times. What you might not have noticed is something else that happened. It clearly says that Jesus knew what people were thinking in their hearts through the Spirit. This was a gift of spiritual discernment.

I knew a prophet once who also had this gift. It was like he could look right through you and know your heart. It was very scary - you'd always try and make sure you were right with God and had confessed all your sins before you went to see him! He would often tell people that God had given him this ability.

God has also given me this gift. I don't tell people about it (I guess that's no longer true if I'm mentioning it here!) because I don't want them to be scared. But when I look in people's eyes I can see people's hearts. Over the years I've come to recognise certain things, as God has told me what they are. I can see things like jealousy, pornography, greed, pride, fear and homosexuality. I can see if people have a mask or are being real. I can see if they are a Christian or not. I can see the spirit of the anti-Christ. But I don't just see negative things. I see love, joy, whole-heartedness for God. I can see other seers and prophets too.

Notes of a Seer

When this first started happening I really didn't know what to do with this information. I found it would affect how I saw the person. So I asked God what to do. He showed me to go beyond what I saw in them now and to see them as He saw them. Full of potential. Having a destiny He had created for them. So often the very area where they are struggling is the same area that will be their strength, their calling, their destiny. I was to flip the negative and see the positive. Where I saw fear God wanted to use them in a big way as ministers of peace. Lust was to be replaced with love. Despair was to be replaced with hope. A divine exchange and a change of thinking.

In the underground Church in China, because they are persecuted and have to be very careful when they meet, they will have people with this gift at the entrance to their meeting place. They will look in people's eyes and discern if they are spies who have come to betray their location or members.

I remember going to a Derek Prince conference many years ago, and they had two women on the entrance doing a similar kind of thing. They were looking into people's eyes to see if they were coming to cause trouble – witches or wizards in disguise. Derek was well known for his deliverance ministry and would often get threats from witches and wizards and those involved in the Occult. They would try and come along to his meetings to cause trouble and disrupt them. I remember their look of shock as they looked into my eyes and I looked right back into theirs. It made me smile.

I was once at a conference and there was a man called Keith Hazel sitting by the side of the stage. I'd heard that he was a major prophet but I'd never met him or heard him speak. I looked into his eyes and saw two things. I saw the strong prophetic. But I also saw a father. I'd never seen that combination before. I didn't know prophets could also be fathers. I thought they were just scary! But as I looked in his eyes I saw what I wanted to be. To be a prophet and a father. I saw that it was possible, because it was who Keith was. It was one of those milestone experiences for me and it's been my heart cry ever since. To be a prophet and a father. Not long after that Keith was "promoted to Glory". I never did get to meet him or hear him. But God still spoke to me through who he was in God.

> But if an unbeliever or someone who does not understand comes in while everybody is prophesying, he will be convinced by all that he is a sinner and will be judged by all, and the secrets of his heart will be laid bare. So he will fall down and worship God, exclaiming, "God is really among you!" (1Co 14:24-25 NIV)

How great is this when a prophecy convicts an unbeliever that they are a sinner because the secrets of their heart have been laid bare and they then become a Christian through it. I have seen this happen and it's a powerful thing.

At one place I was working I'd had a number of opportunities to share my faith with one of my work colleagues who wasn't a Christian. They were quite anti-God and we would end up going round the same loop about suffering and how God couldn't be a God of love. I was at a loss what to do or say. One day as I was praying for this person the Lord gave me a prophetic word for them. I'd never given a prophetic word to a non-Christian before, and wasn't even sure how it would work. But I remembered the passage in 1 Cor 14:24-25 and thought I'd give it a go. I prayed for the right opportunity to share it with them. Eventually it was just me and them in our office, so I gave them the word that I'd written down. I explained to them that because I believe that God is alive and real I also believe that He can speak to us. This was something I believed He'd given me for them. I left the room and quickly went to the toilet to pray! When I came back afterwards, another of my colleagues was standing outside the door to the office with a worried look on her face. "What have you done?!" She asked. I asked her what she meant. She said that she had come back to the office only to find the person I'd given the word to crying in the corner. I told her what I'd done (she was a Christian so she understood about prophecy) and she told me to come back later on. I went off to pray again! That weekend my work colleague became a Christian and also a good friend. She said that there were things in the word that only God would know – the secrets of her heart. For the rest of her life she was a committed Christian and recently got promoted to Glory. I know that one day I will see her again. Don't limit the prophetic to people in your Church. God can speak to anyone – let Him use you as His channel. Let Him speak through you.

There is another school of thought that interprets this passage in a different way and says that the "secrets of their heart" are actually their secret plans or desires. The positive things. Their original destiny from God. That's not that the context for this verse, but I think it's a great way to interpret it. And again, I've seen this happen and it's a powerful thing. When God reveals the secret desires and dreams of a person's heart, it's like an unlocking happens. You can just see them begin to blossom and open up as God speaks life and hope. I shared in my book 'Journey of a Seer' about the "Ice-Cream Cone" prophecy. That was a secret of the person's heart that God knew and revealed. These words can be such an encouragement because only God can know these things. They make people feel known and loved by Him. Which, of course, they are.

Chapter 4: Being Zealous for Spiritual Gifts

> But earnestly desire the higher gifts. (1Co 12:31 ESV)

> Pursue love, and earnestly desire the spiritual gifts, especially that you may prophesy. (1Co 14:1 ESV)

> So, my brothers, earnestly desire to prophesy, and do not forbid speaking in tongues. (1Co 14:39 ESV)

> So also you, since you are zealous of spiritual gifts, seek to abound for the edification of the church. (1Co 14:12 NAS)

Paul encourages the Corinthians to "earnestly desire" the spiritual gifts. The Greek word translated "earnestly desire" in all of the above verses is "zeloo" - ζηλόω [STRONGS 2206]. It's a very strong word, and different Bible translations render it as "earnestly desire", "eagerly desire" or "be zealous of". Desiring the gifts, or seeking the gifts, is not to be a passive thing. It's a very active thing. Paul also stresses that we should not just earnestly desire the spiritual gifts, but we should also pursue love as we express them. And he singles out prophecy in particular as a spiritual gift that we should be desiring. He also gives us the reason why we should be seeking after them. He says that the expression of the gifts is for the edification of the church. Especially the gift of prophecy. He says we are to seek these gifts for the edification of the church. The reason these gifts are given is for the building up of the church – for the edification of the church.

There are some people who say we should be "seeking the giver and not the gift". This sounds very spiritual, but there is no verse in the Bible that actually says this. The people who say this are usually cessationists, that is to say, people who don't believe that the spiritual gifts are for today. If you've got this far in the book then I'm guessing you're not one of those people! But it's important to realise the purpose for which the spiritual gifts have been given. Most of them have been given for the edification of other people in the church. Some of them are for our own edification.

So how do we pursue the gifts? That takes faith. We need to step out in faith and exercise the gifts. And always remember that they are faith expressing itself in love (Gal. 5:6).

A good example of doing this would be Todd White and the gift of healing. I've heard his testimony where he says that he felt that he should pursue the gift of healing. So for just over 3 months he went out every day with his daughter looking for sick people that he could pray for. He would pray every day for 10 people. But not one of the people he prayed for got healed. That was almost 1,000 people without anyone getting healed. Finally, after more than 3 months of seeing no-one he prayed for being healed, he saw his first person get healed. Now, he sees about 70% of the people he prays for get healed. But that only happened because he pursued the gift of healing, because he believed that God wanted to heal people.

Another example of this is Shawn Bolz and the gift of words of knowledge. Similar to Todd, he would deliberately go out and ask God for words of knowledge for people and give them. He aimed for 2 people every day. He would do it with strangers in Starbucks, random people anywhere. He got most of them wrong at the beginning, but as he pursued the gift of words of knowledge he began to get more and more of them right. For him, again like Todd, when he got to about 1,000 people he says he got a lot of them correct.

Knowing that this is how it has worked for both Todd and Shawn I have been deliberately pursuing words of knowledge. I've had a leather bracelet made that says on it "I have secrets for you – God" which I wear every day. I make sure that the text on it is pointing to me, so I can read it and remind myself to continue to pursue. And I have been stepping out with words of knowledge for people. If I get it right (whatever it may be) then I know that God has a prophetic word for that person too. So I'll step out and give that too. When I've got the word of knowledge wrong, most people have been very gracious with me. Some people have also been very encouraging – to pursue it more. So far I've only had one negative reaction – from someone who said I should "seek the giver and not the gift" and that the fact that I'd got it wrong meant that I was deceived. But thankfully the New Testament is a lot more gracious and gives room for us to get these things wrong. It says that we are to judge prophecies. But, unlike the Old Testament, it doesn't instruct us to stone people when they get things wrong. Praise God! There's grace to fail. What's most important is that love is our motive:

> For in Christ Jesus neither circumcision nor uncircumcision has any value. The only thing that counts is faith expressing itself through love. (Gal 5:6 NIV)

Love is our expression. It's important that when we are stepping out in the gifts it is faith expressing itself through love.

Notes of a Seer

Chapter 5: Angelic Encounters

In speaking of the angels he says, "He makes his angels winds, his servants flames of fire." (Heb 1:7 NIV)

The questions I'm asked most frequently are about angels. Questions such as:

• How do I see them?

• What are they like?

• Can you touch them?

If you look through the Bible at all the appearances of angels you can see that they are many and varied. Quite often they appear in a dream or vision (such as with Joseph, Mary's husband – see Mat 1:20).

Sometimes they can appear as a physical form in front of a person such as Gabriel appearing to Zechariah and Mary (see Luke 1). One time I was out in the middle of nowhere and as I looked up I could see this bright shining light. On either side of it were wings flapping back and forth. I knew that it was an angel. As I watched, a small cloud drifted in front of it. When it had passed, the angel had gone! There was nothing else in the sky.

Sometimes they can appear as flames of fire such as with the burning bush before Moses (see Exodus 3:2).

Sometimes they can appear as people (see Hebrews 13:2). One time I found myself as one of the first people at a serious car accident. A car had had a head on collision with another car that had flipped over the central reservation. The front of the car had been smashed in crushing the driver. His wife was next to him, in a daze and in the back were two children and their mother who were trapped and were screaming. I was at a bit of a loss to know what to do. Then a lady appeared behind me and started to tell me what to do: Talk to the wife; make sure she doesn't see her husband next to her; check if the wife has any injuries; and so the dialogue continued. I did all the things she suggested. Other people took the window out of the back of the car and pulled the kids and their mother out. Eventually I carried the wife out with the help of another man and put her safely on the embankment. I turned round to thank the lady for all her advice and support and there was no-one there! There were police cars and an ambulance and the whole site was cleared of people so I would have seen her if she was walking away. But there was no-one. I know that God sent me an angel to help me in that situation and I am so grateful to him.

Sometimes you do not see them but you can see the effect they have on the surroundings, such as the stirring of water at the pool of Bethesda (John 5:4). That was clearly a healing angel because the first person who went into the water after the angel had stirred it would be healed. I shared in 'Journey of a Seer' about the angel push I got from behind me. I couldn't see anything, but I certainly felt the effects and could see the wheat sheaves bobbing back and forth in a small circle behind me. Another time I was in a meeting and as I looked above the people I could see angels flying back and forth above as we worshipped. I lifted my hands up and felt something physically grab hold of my right hand. I could see that it was an angel. Then God told me He wanted us to touch heaven and bring it down to Earth. Heaven on Earth.

Fellow Servants

Are not all angels ministering spirits sent to serve those who will inherit salvation? (Heb 1:1 NIV)

I, John, am the one who heard and saw these things. And when I had heard and seen them, I fell down to worship at the feet of the angel who had been showing them to me. But he said to me, "Do not do it! I am a fellow-servant with you and with your brothers the prophets and of all who keep the words of this book. Worship God!" (Rev 22:8-9 NIV)

Angels are sent by God to serve us. They were even sent to help Jesus at times (Mark 1:13; Luke 22:43). We should ask God to send them and expect that He will do just that. They are the Air Force and we are the Army.

Chapter 6: Open Heaven

Jesus saw Nathanael coming toward him and said of him, "Behold, an Israelite indeed, in whom there is no deceit!" Nathanael said to him, "How do you know me?" Jesus answered him, "Before Philip called you, when you were under the fig tree, I saw you." Nathanael answered him, "Rabbi, you are the Son of God! You are the King of Israel!" Jesus answered him, "Because I said to you, 'I saw you under the fig tree,' do you believe? You will see greater things than these." And he said to him, "Truly, truly, I say to you, you will see heaven opened, and the angels of God ascending and descending on the Son of Man." (John 1:47-51 ESV)

Jesus has a number of words of knowledge about Nathanael when He first meets him. Telling him that he was a true Israelite and that there was no deceit within him was enough to convince him that Jesus knew him – although all that revelation came from the Holy Spirit. But then the Holy Spirit clearly showed Jesus a scene where Nathanael is sitting under the fig tree before Philip calls him. This is clearly a seer operation of the word of knowledge. That, combined with the first word of knowledge, was enough to convince Nathanael the Jesus really is the Messiah, the Son of God, the King of Israel. But there's also a promise here. That promise is that one day Nathanael will see an open heaven.

> When all the people were being baptised, Jesus was baptised too. And as he was praying, heaven was opened and the Holy Spirit descended on him in bodily form like a dove. And a voice came from heaven: "You are my Son, whom I love; with you I am well pleased." (Luke 3:21-22 NIV)

Notes of a Seer

Before Stephen was martyred he saw an open heaven above him:

> But Stephen, full of the Holy Spirit, looked up to heaven and
> saw the glory of God, and Jesus standing at the right hand of
> God. "Look," he said, "I see heaven open and the Son of Man
> standing at the right hand of God." (Act 7:55-56 NIV)

I believe that we, as believers, have an open heaven above us, just
like Jesus, just like Nathanael, just like Stephen. This happened after
Jesus' death on the cross and resurrection. Through the blood of Jesus we now have an open way to the Most Holy Place:

> Therefore, brothers, since we have confidence to enter the
> Most Holy Place by the blood of Jesus, by a new and living
> way opened for us through the curtain, that is, his body, and
> since we have a great priest over the house of God, let us
> draw near to God with a sincere heart in full assurance of
> faith, having our hearts sprinkled to cleanse us from a guilty
> conscience and having our bodies washed with pure water.
> (Heb 10:19-22 NIV)

Above us, there is an open heaven.

Chapter 7: Impartation

> For I long to see you, that I may impart to you some spiritual gift to strengthen you (Rom 1:11 ESV)

In the early Church, there were six teachings that were classed as foundational. They are listed at the beginning of Hebrews 6:

> Therefore, leaving the discussion of the elementary principles of Christ, let us go on to perfection, not laying again the foundation of repentance from dead works and of faith toward God, of the doctrine of baptisms, of laying on of hands, of resurrection of the dead, and of eternal judgment. (Heb 6:1 NKJV)

The six foundational teachings listed here are:

• Repentance from dead works

• Faith towards God

• The doctrine of baptisms (note the plural. They are baptism in water and baptism in the Spirit)

• Laying on of hands

• The resurrection of the dead

• Eternal judgement

In most churches I have ever been in, when dealing with the foundations, they usually stop after the first three. When I was in the Brethren Church I used to hear a lot of preaching about the last one - eternal judgment. But I have never heard a single preach in a

Notes of a Seer

Church on the laying on of hands or the resurrection of the dead. That's pretty amazing, given that the early Church considered them as being foundational. Not to mention the fact that you can't even be a Christian without believing in the resurrection of the dead (see Romans 10:9).

Impartation is usually done through the laying on of hands. A good example of this is with Moses and Joshua:

> And Joshua the son of Nun was full of the spirit of wisdom, for Moses had laid his hands on him. (Deu 34:9 ESV)

Joshua was Moses' assistant – his intern. Moses was full of the spirit of wisdom, so when he laid his hands on Joshua there was an impartation of this anointing onto him.

God also said that He was going to take some of the Spirit that was on Moses and put it on others. This also was an impartation, and you can read about it in Numbers 11:16-29.

> Then the LORD said to Moses, "Gather for me seventy men of the elders of Israel, whom you know to be the elders of the people and officers over them, and bring them to the tent of meeting, and let them take their stand there with you. And I will come down and talk with you there. And I will take some of the Spirit that is on you and put it on them, and they shall bear the burden of the people with you, so that you may not bear it yourself alone. (Num 11:16-17 ESV)

When the Spirit came upon the elders who had gathered they began to prophesy. At the end of this passage you get the great quote from Moses about the prophetic:

> "Oh, that all the LORD'S people were prophets and that the LORD would put His Spirit upon them!" (Num 11:29 NKJV)

Another incident is recorded in 2 Kings2:14. Elisha was Elijah's assistant. When the time came for Elijah to be taken up to heaven Elisha stayed with him up to the very end. Elijah's final question to him was, "What would you like me to do for you?" Elisha replied that he wanted to inherit a double-portion of his spirit. And that's exactly what happened after Elijah was taken up in a chariot and a whirlwind. This was an impartation of the anointing that was on him.

In the New Testament there are a number of times recorded where hands were laid on people for impartation.

Prophetic Presbytery

Neglect not the gift that is in thee, which was given thee by prophecy, with the laying on of the hands of the presbytery. (1Ti 4:14 KJV)

This is an interesting passage. One way of interpreting this is to have something called a "Prophetic Presbytery". The idea of these is that some prophets will lay hands on people and then call out their gifting from God. This will be things like "teacher", "prophet", "evangelist", etc. If you find yourself part of something like this, you need to know the Church denomination or movement you are ministering in. Most denominations and movements don't believe in women apostles, even though there's one clearly mentioned in the Bible called Junias – see Romans 16:7. I find it difficult when I cannot tell a women before me, who clearly has the calling of an apostle, that she is called to be an apostle because her denomination or movement would not permit her to be called that. I'm so grateful for people like Heidi Baker, Jackie Pullinger, Angela Kemm and other women missionaries I've known who are clearly apostles planting churches and moving in the "signs of an apostle" but are never given the honour of the title because of their gender.

I was taught by Godly, Bible believing, men that these women were God's second choice. His first choice had been a man, but because that man hadn't responded to God's call He had sent a women in his place. She was God's second choice.

Later on in life I began to look into these things myself and not take someone else's word for it. I discovered that this wasn't what the Bible taught. Now I don't believe that these women were God's second choice. I believe they were God's first choice.

If there are any women reading this book that have ever been told they were God's second choice I want to tell you that it's not true! I don't think I've ever said that to anyone in the past, but if I have then I am truly sorry and ask you to forgive me. My heart's desire is to see men and women released into their God given calling, whatever that might be.

Laying on of hands

I don't know if you've ever had a go at trying to get someone to lay hands on you for impartation, but it can be a difficult thing! Especially for the more popular people such as Shawn Bolz. They're usually whisked away at the end of a meeting. That's a shame, because I believe impartation through the laying on of hands is a biblical thing and I would love to have had someone like Shawn do that for me. But it's not happened yet. I've simply sought to be faithful to what God has given me and I am always hungry for more.

I have had the opportunity to lay hands on a few people for impartation. I've asked that the Lord would open their eyes and they would begin to see in the spiritual realm. That they would have dreams and visions. Angelic encounters. That God would speak to them powerfully and use them mightily. One or two people I've done this with have begun to experience these afterwards. But it's a lot less than I would like to see. Julian Adams says, "impartation is in seed form" meaning that the person normally needs to grow that seed. He managed to get impartations from Shawn Bolz and James Maloney and they were both significantly important for him.

Someone whom God significantly uses with impartation is Randy Clark. He's the one who opened my eyes to this whole teaching. I've been to see him a number of times and each time he lays hands on me I see an increase in the number of people who get healed that I pray for. His impartation is for healing. It's a shame it's not the prophetic too!

Chapter 8: Birth Prophecies

When it was time for Elizabeth to have her baby, she gave birth to a son. Her neighbours and relatives heard that the Lord had shown her great mercy, and they shared her joy. On the eighth day they came to circumcise the child, and they were going to name him after his father Zechariah, but his mother spoke up and said, "No! He is to be called John." They said to her, "There is no-one among your relatives who has that name." Then they made signs to his father, to find out what he would like to name the child. He asked for a writing tablet, and to everyone's astonishment he wrote, "His name is John." Immediately his mouth was opened and his tongue was loosed, and he began to speak, praising God. The neighbours were all filled with awe, and throughout the hill country of Judea people were talking about all these things. Everyone who heard this wondered about it, asking, "What then is this child going to be?" For the Lord's hand was with him. His father Zechariah was filled with the Holy Spirit and prophesied: "Praise be to the Lord, the God of Israel, because he has come and has redeemed his people. He has raised up a horn of salvation for us in the house of his servant David (as he said through his holy prophets of long ago), salvation from our enemies and from the hand of all who hate us-- to show mercy to our fathers and to remember his holy covenant, the oath he swore to our father Abraham: to rescue us from the hand of our enemies, and to enable us to serve him without fear in holiness and righteousness before him all our days. And you, my child, will be called a prophet of the Most High; for you will go on before the Lord to prepare the way for him, to give his people the knowledge of salvation through the forgiveness of their sins, because of the tender mercy of our God, by which the rising sun will come to us from heaven to shine on those living in darkness and in the shadow of death, to guide our feet into the path of peace." (Luke 1:57-79 NIV)

I believe that those of us who are parents get the right to prophesy over our children when they are born. I did this for each of my kids when they were born. I recorded it on a cassette tape (shows how long ago it was!). We've agreed that when they reach 18 I will give them a copy, written down for them. Last year I got to give my daughter Emily hers. Its amazing how it fitted and how God knew right back at the beginning of her life the plans He had for her. I'm looking forward to giving my two sons theirs when they also get to 18. I'd encourage you to have a go at doing this as your own kids are born too.

Baptism Prophesies

It used to be that when people got baptised in Church there was space given for people to give prophetic words publicly over them. Even now I can remember some of the significant words that were spoken over different people. They were encouraging not just for the person who received them, but also for the whole Church who heard them.

Dedication Prophesies

Now there was a man in Jerusalem called Simeon, who was righteous and devout. He was waiting for the consolation of Israel, and the Holy Spirit was upon him. It had been revealed to him by the Holy Spirit that he would not die before he had seen the Lord's Christ. Moved by the Spirit, he went into the temple courts. When the parents brought in the child Jesus to do for him what the custom of the Law required, Simeon took him in his arms and praised God, saying: "Sovereign Lord, as you have promised, you now dismiss your servant in peace. For my eyes have seen your salvation, which you have prepared in the sight of all people, a light for revelation to the Gentiles and for glory to your people Israel." The child's father and mother marvelled at what was said about him. Then Simeon blessed them and said to Mary, his mother: "This child is destined to cause the falling and rising of many in Israel, and to be a sign that will be spoken against, so that the thoughts of many hearts will be revealed. And a sword will pierce your own soul too." There was also a prophetess, Anna, the daughter of Phanuel, of the tribe of Asher. She was very old; she had lived with her husband seven years after her marriage, and then was a widow until she was eighty-four. She never left the temple but worshipped night and day, fasting and praying. Coming up to them at that very moment, she gave thanks to God and spoke about the child to all who were looking forward to the redemption of Jerusalem. (Luke 2:25-38 NIV)

Dedications are another great time to give space for the prophetic and let people speak words over Children publicly. That's what both Simeon and Anna did for Jesus. Again, they're not just encouraging for the parents but also for the Church who hear them.

Chapter 9: Children who See

When children are young it is not that rare for them to see angels or spiritual things. I have heard testimonies of people who saw when they were children but then an adult, most often their Sunday School teacher, would tell them it was stupid or made up. After that they would stop seeing.

If you have a child who is seeing angels or spiritual things, can I encourage you to encourage them. Even if you don't see anything yourself, listen to what they're saying. I find it helpful to ask them what the things they're seeing make them feel like. They might see swirling lights for angels, or moving dark shadows for demons. The angels will make them feel good. The shadows will make them feel bad. If they're seeing angels then that's really cool! When I would put my children to bed at night I would always pray for them and ask God to surround them with angels whilst they slept and protect them.

One time I was praying for one of my children but couldn't stay to cuddle them to sleep as I normally did. The next day my child told me that he'd asked God to get his angel to give him a cuddle instead. He said he felt the angel holding him and cuddling him and so he was able to go to sleep.

Don't be surprised if a child sees bad things as well as good. When they see a demon, remind them that they can tell them to leave in the name of Jesus. And they have to go. Then tell them to ask God to send some more angels to be with you. To fill the space the demon left.

I do not believe that there is a junior Holy Spirit. I believe that He's the same Holy Spirit, whatever our age. Young or old.

Notes of a Seer

Julian Adams started moving in the prophetic when he was only nine years old! I've seen children even younger than that giving prophetic words. I often go into our childrens work and take a team of people with me to prophesy over the kids and also to encourage them to prophesy over each other. I've had some amazing prophesies given to me over the years by these young children. Don't let age be a barrier to hearing God or to seeing Him move.

Chapter 10: Angel of the Church

To the angel of the church in Ephesus write... (Rev 2:1a NIV)

To the angel of the church in Smyrna write... (Rev 2:8a NIV)

To the angel of the church in Pergamum write... (Rev 2:12a NIV)

To the angel of the church in Thyatira write... (Rev 2:18a NIV)

To the angel of the church in Sardis write... (Rev 3:1a NIV)

To the angel of the church in Philadelphia write... (Rev 3:7a NIV)

To the angel of the church in Laodicea write... (Rev 3:14a NIV)

When the Apostle John was writing letters to the seven Churches he was told to address them to each Church's angel. This is clearly stating that each of those Churches had an angel. As a result of that I believe that, even today, each Church also has an angel.

I mentioned this in my book 'Journey of a Seer' and some people picked up on it. I began to get invites to come to people's churches and tell them what their angel looked like. I've tried to resist that as much as I can, because I don't want to be known as the person who does that. Whenever I go to a church I always ask God to show me their angel and He always has. But the angel is always a portrayal of where they are as a church now, or the destiny that God has for them. Let me give you some examples so you'll understand what I mean.

I went on a trip to Serbia and visited a Roma village that was, quite literally, built in a rubbish dump. When the government knew they had to give the Roma some land where they could live, they gave them some land that was in the middle of their rubbish dump because that was how they saw them. The Roma have cleared away enough for them to be able to live, but they really are the lowest of the low and despised in the eyes of the people around them. The Roma were Muslim, but about 20 years ago a Christian pastor started an outreach amongst them and built a Church. Now a large number of the Roma are Christian.

I had the privilege of visiting their village and also their Church. As I walked about the Roma village I looked up and saw an open heaven over it. I saw angels peering down with awe and wonder and such joy. There was a band playing in the village, accompanying us as we walked along. As I looked up I saw heaven open and the throne of God. Jesus was standing next to the Father, who was seated. But then He got up and started to dance with Jesus to the music. They were having such fun. Then I looked down along the streets of the village and I saw angels dancing and running up and down with children running besides them. I found it all very moving.

When I went to their Church I was blown away by their wholehearted worship and devotion to the Lord. They have so little, yet love Jesus so much.

When I was inside I asked God to show me the angel of their Church. He was this massive angel and his arms and wings were outstretched and he looked magnificent. He had a regal bearing, so full of honour and dignity. The Lord said to me that when He was choosing the angel to assign to this Church there were many who wanted that role, for it was such a privileged position. But the one He chose was special – of a high rank and dignity. This was because He wanted the Roma people who loved Him and worshiped Him to know that they had high honour in His eyes. A special place in His heart.

Chapter 10: Angel of the Church

Once I visited a Church in Leicester. I saw the Angel of the church. He was big and his wings were outstretched. In his arms he was holding a baby. He was enjoying the worship and every now and then would look down at the child and smile and rock it in his arms. I asked the Lord who the child was. He said that it was Isaac. The church was giving birth to an Isaac that was to bring joy to those around. That even in the pastor's old age God was going to fulfil the promises that he had given him - for his church and for himself. There was going to be much laughter and joy in the house of the Lord and around the city and the nation. Joy in the house of the Lord!

I'm sure your own Church has an angel too. Why not ask God to show him to you?

Notes of a Seer

Chapter 11: How do you See?

> Then Elisha prayed and said, "O LORD, please open his eyes
> that he may see." So the LORD opened the eyes of the young
> man, and he saw, and behold, the mountain was full of horses
> and chariots of fire all around Elisha. (2Ki 6:17 ESV)

I have often been asked, "How do you see?" It happens in a few different ways and I will try and explain them.

The first and primary way is in the way Elisha saw in this passage. There is an unseen realm that is around us. It's a spiritual realm. When God shows me things in this way, I clearly see the physical realm in front of me with my physical eyes and at the same time see things from the spiritual realm superimposed on them. An example would be I will look at a building and see sitting on top of the building a big demon, or some angels. I see both the physical and the spiritual at the same time. During a time of worship I might see an angel at the side of the stage, or standing behind someone.

The second way is when I close my eyes. I will usually do this if I want to see above the room I'm in. Again, if I do this in worship it's like the room loses it's roof and I see all that's happening between Earth and heaven at that particular place. One time I was in a meeting and closed my eyes and saw Jesus standing at the front. There was a ladder coming out of the top of His head going up into heaven. I saw angels coming down the ladder down onto Jesus' head and then going out amongst the people in the meeting. They had clearly come to minister to God's people. That really struck me. It wasn't until I got home and looked up John 1:51 that I realised Jesus had said this to Nathanael.

I play bass in our worship band at Church. When I'm standing at the front looking out over the Church I can see what God is doing amongst the people and can often see the angelic above. Often I will close my eyes so I can see Jesus and worship him. I play bass by ear so I don't need the music and when I close my eyes I can play without looking. I simply feel for the frets and go with the flow of the Spirit. Sometimes God will give me a powerful vision as I'm playing with my eyes closed.

I once stayed at a friend's house. They told me they believed there were angels in their house. So I asked the Lord to show me where they were. As I wandered round the house I began to see where they were. One place in particular was my favourite. I went to stand where I could see the angel standing. I was flooded with such peace and light and a real sense of the presence of God, I didn't want to leave. In fact, the whole time I was staying in their house I kept sneaking away to stand in that place and bask in the presence of God.

The third way is with my eyes open. The spiritual things I'm seeing in front of me are so clear and strong I no longer see the physical. It's like it disappears.

Sometimes God will mix it up! I was in a meeting one time and I closed my eyes to see what God was doing on a bigger scale. I saw over to the left this bright, swirling light. When I opened my eyes in looked where I had seen it, there was nothing. So I walked over to the place I'd seen the swirling light. I would alternate with closing my eyes to see it and get an idea of the direction, then opening my eyes and walking towards it. When I got to the place, there was such a heaviness and sense of the presence of God it made me want to lie down and bask in God's presence. When I closed my eyes again, I could see a similar light over to my right. I started walking over to that one, and found someone lying on the floor, basking in the presence of God. I looked out over the room and could see a number of the swirling lights and under each one there was a person lying on the floor! I tried to go back to the place I'd seen the first swirling light, but now there was someone lying on the floor. Next time when I see those lights I'll lie down straight away.

Notes of a Seer

light, but now there was someone lying on the floor. Next time when I see those lights I'll lie down straight away.

Chapter 12: Rooms of Heaven

In my Father's house are many rooms; if it were not so, I would have told you. (John 14:2 NIV)

There are many different rooms in heaven and at different times the Lord has shown some of them to me. I mentioned some of these in 'Journey of a Seer': The 'Provision Room', the 'Destiny Room', the 'Healing Room', the 'Music Room' and the 'Room of Restoration'. One thing I didn't mention about the 'Room of Restoration' was that God told me that whenever I saw a door above a person, this was to show that there was a 'Room of Restoration' for them and that I should ask God to show me what was inside. It wasn't until a couple of years later that I actually saw a door over someone, together with an object. I prophesied over the person from the object, then I asked God to show me what was behind the door. The door opened and I was in a room. I could see what looked like a filing cabinet in the corner, with one of the drawers pulled out. Inside the drawer were lots of files, detailing all the things that had happened to this person in the past few years. It was like one thing, after another thing, after another. I described to the person what I was seeing and how it had been a season of what seemed like a never ending number of things that had been going wrong and attacks. Of things that were coming against them. But God wanted them to know that this season was ending and that he was going to renew them. That as the number of their days so was their strength going to be.

I was prophesying all of this whilst looking at the unfolding vision above her head. I had no idea what kind of impact it was having on her. When the vision finished I looked down to her and she was completely undone. When I saw this I was overwhelmed too. When I chatted with her after the meeting she said it had been so true of the past few years and that she was encouraged by what God was going to do.

Now I'm on the lookout for more of those doors! I believe God wants to restore a lot of things to the children of God that the enemy has stolen – the children's bread.

I also wanted to share about some other rooms I've visited.

War Room

One time I was in the Spirit and an angel guided me to a room. In the middle of the room there was a massive map of a part of the world. It covered all of Europe and the Balkans. There were angels standing round the map, and the Father was consulting with Jesus. As I looked at the map I could see Satan's plan for this part of the world unfolding before me. I saw a movement sweeping from East to West. As people moved countries began building up walls and planting flags. Each of these flags were black and red. The countries believed they were making themselves stronger because of their walls. But actually this was making them weaker, because they were becoming independent. This was Satan's strategy because it was preparation for his real plan, which was to conquer each of these countries from East to West. Things looked desperate and it seemed like his plan was going to work. But then God showed me His plan. I saw Christians reaching out to each other and holding hands. These hands spread across the whole of the map. They crossed borders. Crossed countries. There was strength as they held each other. I saw power, like lightning, sparking up and down the lines. Christians were standing with each other. Helping each other. Friends. Brothers and sisters.

Wisdom Room

One time I was shown the 'Wisdom Room'. Inside this room there were lots of spheres. Each of these spheres had names written on them. One had written on it 'Nicaragua'. This was wisdom for a whole nation. It was available for the taking. I saw people praying for different kinds of wisdom and angels would be dispatched to this room and would pick up the sphere for the thing they were asking wisdom for. There were other nations there too. I also saw one name 'Police'. It was wisdom for the police force. God promises us wisdom to those who ask Him:

> If any of you lacks wisdom, he should ask God, who gives generously to all without finding fault, and it will be given to him. (Jam 1:5 NIV)

Notes of a Seer

Chapter 13: Know Your Sphere

We, however, will not boast beyond measure, but within the limits of the sphere which God appointed us-- a sphere which especially includes you. For we are not overextending ourselves (as though our authority did not extend to you), for it was to you that we came with the gospel of Christ; not boasting of things beyond measure, that is, in other men's labours, but having hope, that as your faith is increased, we shall be greatly enlarged by you in our sphere, to preach the gospel in the regions beyond you, and not to boast in another man's sphere of accomplishment. (2Co 10:13-16 NKJV)

Paul here talks about the sphere that God had appointed him. I believe that the prophetic also operates within spheres and its important for us to discover what that sphere is. These spheres can be:

- Places we're called to

- Individuals we're called to

- People groups we're called to

- One (or many) of the seven mountains of society (I will explain that in a minute)

- Issues we're called to

Places

Some people are called to serve a particular place. This might be abroad. This might be in their current country. You might have friends who are living in a particular country and as you pray for them you find a growing burden not just for them but also for that nation. God starts to speak to you about that nation and His plans for it. You might find God starts doing that for your own nation as you pray for it. He starts speaking to you about His plans. One verse I always find useful in this is Amos 3:7

> Surely the sovereign Lord does nothing without revealing His plans to His servants the prophets

It might be more local than a whole nation. It might just be a city. Again, God starts speaking to you about His plans for that city.

Individuals

Sometimes we can be called to serve particular people. I have had seasons in my life where I have felt called to serve particular people. Sometimes that can be in a mentoring kind of relationship, similar to Elisha and Elijah. Other times God calls me to stand alongside leaders, to intercede for them and also to hear God for them. I've also found that there's a strong pull whenever I'm around an Apostle. Apostles and Prophets are supposed to work together. In fact, they're foundational:

> Consequently, you are no longer foreigners and aliens, but fellow-citizens with God's people and members of God's household, built on the foundation of the apostles and prophets, with Christ Jesus himself as the chief cornerstone. In him the whole building is joined together and rises to become a holy temple in the Lord. (Eph 2:19-21 NIV)

People groups

Sometimes we can be called to serve a particular people group. These people can be in more than one location. An example of this could be Chinese people, wherever they are located in the world. Again, God can start speaking to you about them and revealing His plans to you.

Seven mountains of society

Loren Cunningham, the founder of YWAM, wrote about the seven mountains of society in his book 'Making Jesus Lord':

1. The family

2. Spirituality

3. Education

4. Media

5. Entertainment

6. Economy

7. Government

Again, one of these (or many) could be areas you particularly feel called to serve. God will be speaking to you about them and His plans.

Issues

These can be things such as:

• Injustice

• Sex trafficking

• Racism

• Abortion

• Corruption

Notes of a Seer

- The poor

- The homeless

- Orphans/widows

As we see these things happening God starts speaking to us about them. He not only sees them as wrong but stirs you up to do something about it and speak up and speak out for those who often can't speak for themselves.

Summary

It's important to realise that the prophetic can be so much more than simply giving words to individuals. God has plans for lots of different things and He wants to reveal them to us. Take time out to seek His heart for some of the things I've listed here and see if God is maybe wanting you to use you in different spheres.

Chapter 14: Understanding what you See

Then Amaziah said to Amos, "Get out, you seer! Go back to the land of Judah. Earn your bread there and do your prophesying there. Don't prophesy any more at Bethel, because this is the king's sanctuary and the temple of the kingdom." Amos answered Amaziah, "I was neither a prophet nor a prophet's son, but I was a shepherd, and I also took care of sycamore-fig trees. But the LORD took me from tending the flock and said to me, 'Go, prophesy to my people Israel.'" (Amos 7:12-15 NIV)

Amos is one of my favourite characters in the Bible. He was a shepherd who was tending his sheep in the land of Judah and God called him to be a prophet to the people of Israel. By the time Amos was prophesying the people of Israel were in a pretty bad way and had strayed far from God. Amos is called both a seer and a prophet in this passage.

Twice in his book Amos records how God showed him something and then gets him to ask God questions about what he is seeing. The question God asks is "what do you see?" (Amos 7:8; 8:2). God asked Jeremiah the same question as He showed him things in visions (Jer 1:11,13; 24:3). And God did the same with Zechariah, asking Him the same question as He also showed him things in visions (Zech 4:2; 5:2).

I know it would be simpler for God to simply speak the words to the prophet and for them to speak the words to the people. We'd simply be His mouthpiece. But when you see Him interacting with His prophets there's a dialogue going on. He wants them to ask questions. He wants them to draw the words out of Him. This is because the prophetic comes out of our relationship with the Father and our identity as His sons and daughters. We have access to the throne of God through the shed blood of Jesus and can stand in His presence and hear Him speak. We can also ask Him questions.

So when God shows us something we must go back to God and ask Him what it means. Just because you've seen something before and God told you what it meant, don't assume that it will mean the same thing the next time. For example, a key might mean God wants to unlock something within a person. But the next time it might mean God wants to use them to unlock others. All understanding comes from the Holy Spirit.

If you're asking God for a word for somebody then there are some questions you can always start to ask God about them:

- How's their relationship with you?
- What do you love about them?
- What connects them the most to you? Is it worship? Healing? The Bible? Soaking? The Prophetic?
- How about their family?
- What do you want to encourage them about?
- What's going in their family?
- Their extended family?
- Do they have kids?
- Wife?
- What about their career?
- Are they a housewife/househusband? Student? Businessman?
- How do they spend their life?
- How are they called to serve you?
- In business? In the Church?
- What's their favourite colour?
- Anything else?

These are all good questions to be asking God about the person. Listen to what He says or look at what He shows you.

Chapter 14: Understanding what you See

God loves to communicate. When God sent His Son, He sent Him as His Word. Our job is simply to listen or look and then to speak out what we hear or see. What's important is that when we do this, we do this in love. Love must always be our motive and our expression.

Notes of a Seer

Chapter 16: Spiritual Warfare

Put on the whole armour of God, that you may be able to stand against the schemes of the devil. For we do not wrestle against flesh and blood, but against the rulers, against the authorities, against the cosmic powers over this present darkness, against the spiritual forces of evil in the heavenly places. Therefore take up the whole armour of God, that you may be able to withstand in the evil day, and having done all, to stand firm. Stand therefore, having fastened on the belt of truth, and having put on the breastplate of righteousness, and, as shoes for your feet, having put on the readiness given by the gospel of peace. In all circumstances take up the shield of faith, with which you can extinguish all the flaming darts of the evil one; and take the helmet of salvation, and the sword of the Spirit, which is the word of God, praying at all times in the Spirit, with all prayer and supplication. To that end keep alert with all perseverance, making supplication for all the saints (Eph 6:11-18 ESV)

Most Christians put a full stop in the middle of verse 12 – "For we do not wrestle." But the fact is, when we were born again and became a Christian we were rescued from the kingdom of darkness and brought into the kingdom of light - the Kingdom of God. And that kingdom is already at war with Satan's kingdom. The war was declared before you were born.

My Mum was born in 1940. At that time Britain was at war with Germany - it was the Second World War. Even though the war was declared before she was born, she was immediately born into war. The children born at that time were known as "War Babies". That's the same for us as Christians. When we were born again we became "War Babies". The war already started many years ago. Satan doesn't wait for us to grow up and mature. He starts the warfare right away.

Notes of a Seer

Because of this, it's important that we aren't ignorant of Satan's schemes (see 2 Co 2:11). That was one of the four things I told you previously that we weren't to be ignorant of. So what are his schemes against us and what can we do to protect ourselves? Thankfully, Paul describes in this passage where the attacks will be coming from. They come from the spiritual forces of evil in the heavenly places. The question you might be asking at this point is, "How can there be any evil in the heavenly realms?" To help explain this, you need to understand that there is more than one heaven.

The Hebrew word for heaven, "shamayim" שָׁמַיִם [STRONGS 08064], is never used in the singular. It is always plural. The Bible talks about a first heaven (Rev 21:1) and a third heaven (2 Co 12:2). So it seems reasonable to assume there is also a second heaven that is between the two - although the Bible never explicitly mentions this by name. The second heaven is the heavenly realm that the spiritual forces of evil occupy. These forces have titles:

• Principalities- some translations use the word "rulers". The Greek word is "arche" ἀρχή [STRONGS 746]. It's the same prefix used for archangels.
•   Authorities – this is the Greek word "exousia" ἐξουσία [STRONGS 1849] and is used for governmental rule
•   Powers – this is the Greek word "kosmokrator" κοσμοκράτωρ [STRONGS 2888]

There are people who say there is no Biblical precedent to be engaging in spiritual warfare with any of these spiritual forces of evil. But that's not what Paul is saying here. If you're participating in a wrestling match it's not a spectator sport! But we need to be wise about how we do this and when. I'll come back to this a bit later.

Since we are in a war and our enemy is already attacking us, it's vitally important that we put on our armour so we can stand.

I shared a story in 'Journey of a Seer' about the time we had the Buddhist monks chanting next door to us when we living in Tibet and how as a result of that I began to put on my Spiritual Armour every day. I might not be in Tibet any longer, but I'm still in a war. I have some proclamations that I declare for each of the piece of armour.

If you've never done any proclamations before then I'd really encourage you to try them. You take some verses that have a certain truth. Then you personalise it. Then you speak it out.

I'll give you an example with a proclamation about peace. The original verses look like this:

> Do not be anxious about anything, but in everything, by prayer and petition, with thanksgiving, present your requests to God. And the peace of God, which transcends all understanding, will guard your hearts and your minds in Christ Jesus. (Phi 4:6-7 NIV)

That's a great promise! To make it a proclamation, change the words to apply to yourself. This then becomes:

> I am not anxious about anything, but in everything, by prayer and petition, with thanksgiving, I present my requests to God. And the peace of God, which transcends all understanding, guards my heart and my mind in Christ Jesus.

Having made it a proclamation, you now need to speak this out, believing that what it says is true. It's straight out of Scripture. But often we can struggle to believe it when we make it personal like this. Don't listen to Satan's lies. Know the truth. Proclaim the truth. It will set you free.

I have proclamations for all the different pieces of the armour. I speak them out as I picture myself putting that particular piece on. I'll give you examples as I go through the different pieces. I'll put all those proclamations together in an Appendix so you can say them too if you're interested.

Putting on the armour

I always start with the following proclamation, before I put any piece on. For me it sets the context:

> The hour has come for me to wake up from my slumber, because my salvation is nearer now than when I first believed. The night is nearly over, the day is almost here. So I put aside the deeds of darkness and put on the armour of light. I clothe myself with the Lord Jesus Christ, and do not think about how to gratify the desires of the flesh. (based on Rom 13:11-14)

Breastplate of righteousness

I know it's not the first piece in Ephesians 6, but it's usually where I start. What does that mean, "the breastplate of righteousness"? The breastplate protects the heart, so it's clearly important. I believe that our righteousness comes through the blood of Jesus. So for this piece of armour I have a number of proclamations to do with the blood of Jesus. First I start by declaring what the blood of Jesus has done for me:

• Through the blood of Jesus I am redeemed out of the hands of the Devil
• Through the blood of Jesus all my sins are forgiven
• Through the blood of Jesus I am continually being cleansed from all my sin
• Through the blood of Jesus I am justified, made righteous, just-as-if-I'd never sinned
• Through the blood of Jesus I am sanctified, made holy, set apart to God
• Through the blood of Jesus I have boldness to enter into the presence of God
• The blood of Jesus continually cries out continually to God in heaven on my behalf

Having done that I then run through the proclamations that declare each of these truths.

Helmet of Hope

The next piece of armour I put on is the helmet of hope. Ephesians 6 talks about the helmet of salvation, so why do I change it to the helmet of hope? There's a parallel passage in 1 Thess that also describes the breastplate and the helmet:

> But since we belong to the day, let us be self-controlled, putting on faith and love as a breastplate, and the hope of salvation as a helmet. (1Th 5:8 NIV)

Here the helmet is called the helmet of the hope of salvation. So I see that as the helmet of hope. The helmet is to protect the head – to protect our mind. And the important protector of our minds is the hope of God.

Again, I proclaim some things about hope from the Bible at the same time as imagining putting on a helmet. I usually do this indoors, but if I'm outdoors and forget it must look really strange to other people as I put on an invisible helmet with my hands!

Shoes of peace

Paul tells us to put on our feet the shoes of the readiness for the Gospel. We must be prepared to travel wherever He wants to take us to tell people the good news about Jesus. This gospel is called the gospel of peace. For these shoes I have a number of proclamations about peace.

Belt of Truth

I go through three sets of proclamations for the belt of truth. These are for the Father, the Son and the Holy Spirit. All of them are described as speaking the truth.

Shield of Faith

The shield of faith is to protect us from the fiery darts of the evil one. These are the accusations that the Devil sends our way. For me, I picture myself lifting up a shield and saying this:

I love you Lord God and I trust you.
I love you Lord God and I trust you.
I love you Lord God and I trust you.

There are times when you don't understand what God is doing. Times when just standing seems so hard, let alone trying to contemplate moving forward. At those times I lift up my shield and I say those words. They remind me that God is in control of my life. I love Him. I trust Him completely. He knows what He's doing. My life is in His hands.

Sword of the Spirit

The sword of the Spirit is the Word of God – the Bible. I speak out some proclamations about the Bible.

Pray in the Spirit

Paul's exhortation ends with encouraging us to pray in the Spirit. I'll end with praying in tongues.
Once I've put on my armour I'm ready to start praying for people, as Paul also encourages us to do.

Engaging in Spiritual Warfare

I've talked about how important it is to put on our armour each day. But are we to also engage in Strategic Level Warfare? This used to be a big thing many years ago and caused a lot of controversy. I don't hear people talking about it these days. That's interesting, because those spiritual forces of evil in the heavenly realms haven't gone away.

One time when we were in Tibet a member of our team needed to get a permit so they could continue to study Tibetan at the local university. In the Tibetan pantheon of gods there is a demon whose sole job is to stop non-Buddhists from learning the Tibetan language. When we discovered this we specifically targeted that demon one evening, commanding him to release the permit that our team member needed, in the name of Jesus. The very next day he got his permit!

Being Strategic

The original religion of Tibet was something called Bön. When the Buddhists were trying to bring their religion into Tibet they didn't have a lot of success for many years. Then one day, the wife of a Tibetan king had a dream. In that dream she saw the demoness of the Bön religion lying over the land. Then she was shown to build Buddhist temples at all the key parts of this demoness. Her heart, her knees, etc. If you want to see it, do a Google Images search for "demoness of Tibet". They used to have this picture hanging in the Summer Palace in Lhasa. The strategy that was revealed to her was to pin the demon down with the Buddhist temples and that in this way they would be able to subdue the Bön religion and Buddhism would triumph. They used this strategy and it did in fact work.

Why do I use this example? Because I believe that God can give us strategies too for bringing the Gospel to nations, to cities, to people. But we need to be sure it is from Him before we engage in any kind of warfare at this strategic level. We will need lots of protection (I usually ask for lots of big angels) and wisdom from Him.

In Jesus we have authority over all principalities, authorities, powers and demons of all kinds. That's great news! But I've seen far too many people come to grief over the years who have engaged these things when God wasn't leading them to do it. Know His leading. It's powerful stuff. Handle with care!

Argentina had an amazing revival and one of the leading evangelists was a person called Carlos Anacondia. He became famous for using the phrase "Listen to me Satan!" He would tell him to take his hands of the people. When he did this in his campaigns quite literally all hell would break loose. People who were manifesting demons would be taken out to a tent where they would then be delivered. People wouldn't just become Christians but they would also get clean. Because of this the attrition rate of people who became Christians at his campaigns was very low. He would also make sure to involve the local Churches.

An Impartation

I was at a Randy Clark conference recently and went forward for an impartation. As I was standing at the front with my eyes closed my left leg started to shake. I don't normally get manifestations when the Holy Spirit comes on me, so this was unusual. After a little bit the shaking stopped. Then it started again, but this time it wasn't just my left leg but also my left hand and arm. Again, after a little bit, it stopped. Then God asked me a question: "How undignified was I prepared to become in order for God anoint me powerfully?" I told Him I was prepared to be as undignified as necessary. Whatever it takes. I wanted more. After I'd said that my left leg, left arm, right leg and right arm started shaking. In fact, all of me was shaking. At that same moment I saw this massive demon appear in front of me. Boy did that stir me up! As I'm shaking massively I started shouting out in tongues against the demon that's in front of me, doing warfare against it and commanding it to leave. It must have been quite a sight to those around me because a member of the ministry team came alongside me saying whatever demon was inside me should come out. But the demon wasn't inside me, it was outside and I was doing battle with it. Then the demon disappeared because I had driven it away in the name of Jesus. At the same time the shaking stopped and I was surrounded by bright white light. I was in heaven and Jesus was beside me. I felt such peace in His presence. That's when He told me that He had anointed me with power to drive out demons and destroy all the works of the enemy. Amen!

Expelling Demons

Jesus cast demons out of people and his disciples did it too. In Mark 16 it's one of the things we're told to do as disciples (Mark 16:17). I would highly checking out the books in the recommend reading section. Even better, if you can get someone to mentor you in this that's great! It's not complicated, but you need to be wise about how you go about doing it. You need to know that your authority to cast demons out doesn't increase with the volume of your voice! It also doesn't increase with the number of people speaking out. If you're in a group, only one of you should do the speaking. The rest can pray in tongues.

A good model to follow for deliverance is Pablo Bottari's Ten-step model. He developed it from doing evangelistic campaigns with Carlos Anacondia. He was the man in charge of the tent were people were taken when they began to manifest demons. The goal of the model is to not just expel any demons but also to close any doors through which they gained access in the first place and then to help the person to keep those doors closed. Deliverance is most effective when done in a team. Only one person should be in charge at a time. That person will do all the talking and if needed any touching. The other members of the team should pray silently and talk with the leader quietly. You can rotate the leadership during the time of ministry but always make sure it's just the one person. Some of the steps can be quite painful to process so don't feel it all has to be done in one session. If needs be you can offer to have the person go home and come back at a later time.

Here are the Ten Steps:

1. Give the individual priority

Always maintain a loving attitude. Make love your goal. Be encouraging. Move to a quiet place if possible and invite the Holy Spirit to come and be present.

2. If a spirit manifests, make it be quiet

If a spirit manifests, tell it to be quiet in the name of Jesus! Be persistent. This might take a while but don't stop until it is quiet. Only the leader should do this. Don't shout louder. An increase in volume doesn't equal an increase in authority.

3. Establish and maintain communication with the person

You must have the co-operation of the person you are ministering to. Ask them if they can hear you.

4. Ask the person what they want freedom from

It's really important to establish that the person actually wants freedom from the bondage(s). Sometimes they're not ready to let them go. If that's the case, then there's no point in carrying on. For these people simply bless them and finish the session.

5. Make sure the person has accepted Jesus as their Lord and Saviour

If they haven't, then lead them in a prayer of salvation. If they're not prepared to do that, then simply bless them and finish the session.

6. Interview the person to discover what led to the bondage(s)

This can be through events or relationships. Quite often forgiveness will be required. A good help in identifying these things are thinking about body, soul and spirit. Body can include sexual sins, addictions, etc. Soul can include things to do with our emotions such as fears, trauma, etc. Spirit can include involvement in the occult, Witchcraft, etc.

7. Lead the person in closing the door(s) through which the spirit(s) entered

There's four things to do:

- Forgive – if needed
- Repent
- Renounce – the person needs to do this audibly
- Break the bondage – the leader should do this

8. Cast out the unclean spirit(s) in the name of Jesus

Command the unclean spirit to come out of the person in the name of Jesus.

9. Have the person thank Jesus for their deliverance

If this isn't possible because there's more spirits manifesting, then go back to step 2.

10. Have the person ask the Holy Spirit to fill them

It's vitally important that having cleaned out space you ask the Holy Spirit to come and fill the places formerly occupied by the unclean spirits. If more manifestations start to happen at this point, go back to stage 2.

Notes of a Seer

Chapter 17: Word of God

All Scripture is God-breathed and is useful for teaching, rebuking, correcting and training in righteousness (2Ti 3:16 NIV)

If we want to move and grow in the prophetic then we need to know the Word of God – the Bible. The Bible is God-breathed. If you want to know the language of God then you need to know the Bible. It's how He speaks. It's His words. His grammar. His vocabulary.

I would encourage everyone to read the Bible at least once in their life. If you've never done that yet then why not get a "Bible in a year" Bible, or use a plan with your favourite Bible app? There are words of love that God wants to speak to you that you haven't heard yet.

When my wife and I were first dating we ended up in different places for a while. I would write to her every day and she would write back. When I got those letters I didn't skim through to get the main points. I didn't jump to the end to see the outcome. I savoured every word because they were written to me by someone I loved. That's what the Bible is for you. Savour every word.

But don't stop at just once. My favourite all time movie is called "Ferris Bueller's Day Off". It's from the eighties and I love it. I have seen that film so many times I can repeat most of the dialogue. Yet every time I watch it I see something new. Something I hadn't seen before. That's what happens when you read through the Bible again. I guarantee you'll see something new. That's also the reason why I don't highlight my Bible. I found that when I highlighted verses the next time I read a passage I would automatically be drawn to the verses I'd highlighted. If you don't highlight the Bible then it's always a fresh book. Let the Holy Spirit speak to you afresh. Of course, if you like to highlight, you could always just keep buying a new Bible every now and then to keep it fresh!

In China there has been a massive revival since the Cultural Revolution. The revival has taken place in the underground Church amidst great persecution which still continues to this day. The only way to get a Bible is to be a member of the registered Church. Because the registered Church says that the government is more important than God Christians don't join it and instead meet secretly as part of the underground Church. What this means is that lots of Chinese Christians don't have their own Bibles. So they will copy Scriptures by hand and memorise huge portions of the Bible. They place a high value on the word of God. When I see the different Bibles on my bookshelves it makes me think of my Chinese Christian brothers and sisters who do without. It makes me grateful for what God has given me and I pray that God will also provide each of them with their own copy of God's word.

Bible Memorisation

Do not let this Book of the Law depart from your mouth; meditate on it day and night, so that you may be careful to do everything written in it. Then you will be prosperous and successful. (Jos 1:8 NIV)

That's quite a promise to those who know Scripture and meditate on it. Prosperity and success! Memorising passages of the Bible is a great thing to do. It also helps with Bible Meditation, which I'll talk about in a bit. As we memorise passages, it's like they get inside us. We don't need to open the Bible to read out the verses. We can simply speak them out. This helps again with the prophetic as we speak out His words. When I started memorising the Bible I used something called the "Topical Memory System" by the Navigators. This had verses written down on card and a little wallet you could put them into. You can still buy this. But now I use an app on my phone which is much simpler and means you don't have to carry all those cards around with you. The app I use is called "Bible Memory Pro". I'm sure there are others too.

Bible Meditation

Before I became a Christian I used to practise Eastern Meditation. With that, you empty your mind and it's quite relaxing. When I became a Christian I stopped doing that. But the Bible talks about meditation too (Josh 1:8). The big difference with Bible meditation is that instead of emptying our minds, we fill them with the Word of God. This is where memorising the Bible is helpful. As you continue to repeat verses and fill your mind with them, they start sinking down into your heart. You don't even need to memorise Scripture to do this. Pick a verse or a few verses (not too many). Keep reading and re-reading them, asking the Holy Spirit to speak them to your heart. If you've never done it before, I'd encourage you to give it a go.

After I had my heart bypass I found it difficult to get to sleep as any movement caused me pain and would wake me up. So I bought an MP3 player and a pillow speaker and recorded some things I would listen to as I tried to get to sleep. When I woke up again in the middle of the night I'd start it again. I put a book of the Bible onto it and listen to that. At the moment I'm listening to Hebrews. It's a great way of meditating on Scripture. Joshua 1:8 says we should be doing that day and night. The only drawback is that when I'm listening to music in shuffle mode on my phone during the day I have to be careful it doesn't pick a chapter from Hebrews. As soon as it comes on I just want to fall asleep. Not great if you're driving a car or sitting at your desk in work!

Chapter 18: Hear and Obey

But they did not obey nor incline their ear, but made their neck stiff, that they might not hear nor receive instruction. (Jer 17:23 NKJV)

When God speaks to you, what do you do with it? Do you write it down somewhere? Do you keep it in a journal? It's important to make a record of the things God has spoken to you. If someone gives you a prophetic word verbally, try and make sure you record it. If you've got your mobile phone with you, there's usually an app you can use (like Voice Memo on an iPhone) to do this. Afterwards, make sure you take time to transcribe the word. Write it down.

But after you have done this, what do you do next? What do you do with what God has spoken to you?

Listen

The Hebrew word for "Listen" is "shama" שָׁמַע [STRONGS 8085]. It doesn't just mean to listen but it is also used for "hear" and "obey". The implication of this word is "to hear is to obey".

A good example of this is when God first speaks to Samuel as a small boy in the temple. God keeps calling him, but he thinks it's Eli the priest. Eventually Eli twigs what's going on and tells Samuel to say to God, "Speak, for your servant is listening [shama]" (see 1 Sam 3:11). He says he is God's servant. For Samuel, to hear was to obey.

Two Paths

When God speaks to us it's the start of a journey. There are actually two different paths and the point where the paths fork is how we listen. Listening is the fork in the road. In fact, listening is one of the most important things we do as Christians. And listening starts with our attitude. There are actually two different attitudes: the "inclined ear" and the "stiff neck".

Inclined Ear

My son, give attention to my words; Incline your ear to my sayings. Do not let them depart from your eyes; Keep them in the midst of your heart; For they are life to those who find them, And health to all their flesh. (Pro 4:20-22 NKJV)

What does the Bible mean when it talks about inclining your ear? This actually speaks of an attitude of humility, of a willingness to obey. A good example of this is Mary, the mother of Jesus. When the angel Gabriel appears before her and tells her she is going to bear the Son of God she says:

And Mary said, "Behold, I am the servant of the Lord; let it be to me according to your word." (Luke 1:38 ESV)

Like Samuel, she says she is God's servant. For Mary too, to hear was to obey.

Inclined Ear Outcome

As we travel down the path of the inclined ear we find there are two great results. First we find that our hearing is sharpened and it becomes easier to listen to God. Secondly we find our hearts become softer towards God and other people. We then loop back to that fork in the road again, but this time we've gone higher. We're travelling on an upwardly empowering spiral of spiritual growth. It becomes easier to hear God and we're more receptive to doing what He says.

Stiff Neck

And he also rebelled against King Nebuchadnezzar, who had made him swear an oath by God; but he stiffened his neck and hardened his heart against turning to the LORD God of Israel. (2Ch 36:13 NKJV)

A good example of stiffening your neck when God speaks a word to you is Zedekiah and his reaction to the words God spoke to him through the prophet Jeremiah. The Bible says that he "stiffened his neck" and "hardened his heart". These two things go hand in hand. Stiffening your neck speaks of pride, of arrogance. Rather than humbling themselves when God's word comes and obeying Him, these people choose to not obey. They also harden their hearts.

There's another, more subtle, way of not obeying God. That is to delay obedience and put it off until another day. But there's an important thing to remember when we do this. There comes a point where delayed obedience simply becomes dis-obedience.

Stiff Neck Outcome

As we listen to God and choose to disobey we find that our hearing becomes duller and our hearts become harder. We loop back to that fork again, but this time we've gone lower. We're travelling on a downward dive of despondent dullness. It becomes harder to hear God and we're less inclined to do what He says.

Keeping on the good path

So how do we keep on the good path? How do we keep on the path of the "inclined ear"? It's quite simple, really. Do what He says and do it as quickly as you can. If you can, tell someone else about what God has said to you. Be accountable. Make sure you tell someone who will make sure you do it. In my experience, tell a South African. They'll always make sure you do it!

Coffee Time

One thing I do is when I sit down to have coffee with someone I know I'll ask them two questions:
- What is God saying to you at the moment?
- What are you doing about it?

I'd encourage you to find a friend who can do that for you too.

Chapter 19: When things go wrong

I'm very conscious that I have been very careful in choosing my examples and stories and they can give the impression that I never get things wrong. But that's really not true! What I want to talk about in this chapter is some of the things I got wrong and what the Lord taught me through those experiences. Even the most anointed prophets alive today don't have a 100% success rate if they were honest with you. I certainly don't either.

When I first started getting words I was very much focused on speaking truth and there was very little, if any, love. I cringe now when I think of some of the things I said and am quite ashamed of my attitude at the time. But I discovered the importance of love and now that is always my goal whenever I share a word.

The problem was when I gave a word that turned out to be wrong and I hadn't given it in love. That was a really painful experience, both for the person I gave the word to and also for me. I quickly learned to minister in love. If you start with an attitude of love that means that if you get it wrong at least they'll feel loved. Make love your goal.

As you begin to step out you need to work out if it is the Lord prompting you to prophesy or if it's just you. Sometimes He can show you something but He doesn't want you to share it publically. He might want you to use it for prayer. Ask Him which it is. Always ask Him.

Whenever I've got it wrong I will go back over the situation again. I will ask questions such as: what was I feeling? What made me think it was God? Was there any part of it that was right or was it all off? What should I avoid next time? What would I do different? Learn from your failures.

If you give someone a word and it has timescales of any kind then try and check back with the person at a later date and see if what you prophesied happened. If it didn't, then apologise and explain that your motives where good and you genuinely believed you were hearing from God, but you clearly got it wrong this time. Tell them that you're sorry. It's really important that we are accountable for the word's we give.

I can still remember, years after I gave them, quite a number of the words I got wrong. On the other hand, I can't remember most of the ones I got right. It's really important that we learn from our mistakes. That we are accountable where we can be. That we don't let our failures stop us from stepping out and trying again. Given that sometimes you'll get them wrong, don't forget what I've mentioned already. Make love your goal.

A few times in my life the Lord has given me difficult words for people, including words of rebuke. I find them hard, and I will always ask God to confirm them by giving me a sign. One time I had a particularly difficult word to give to an eldership and it was talking about a friend of mine in the past tense. This friend wasn't even ill at the time. So I asked God to give me a sign to confirm the word. If the sign came true then I knew the word was true and I would then give it to the elders. The sign I was given was this, "Unto us a child is born, unto us a son is given". I thought that was a strange sign, but I held onto the word anyway. A few months after I got the word my friend got sick with what turned out to be a brain tumour. He rapidly went downhill and Christmas was approaching. The week before Christmas it suddenly struck me about the sign. It was the Christmas message. I knew at that moment that my friend was going to die at Christmas and that the word God had given me really was for the elders. The final confirmation, if it was needed, was the preach that Sunday was from Isaiah 9. That was the hardest word I've ever given. If you're unsure about the word God has given you then ask Him to give you a sign. If the sign is confirmed then you know it's from Him. If the sign isn't confirmed then let it go and assume you've got it wrong this time.

At that same Church I got another word. There were three elders at the time, but this word was for just two of them. It said not to worry about what had just happened to them. That God knew it was going to happen and that He was with them and would help them as they moved forward. I wrote the word down and took it to the mid-week meeting wondering what to do with this strange word. In the middle of the meeting one of the elders blew up. He was really upset and angry and said he couldn't work with the other two elders any-more and was leaving the Church and being an elder. He stormed out of the meeting and that was the last we saw of him. After he'd gone I gave the other two elders the word. I told them I'd got it earlier and hadn't understood it, but now it made complete sense. It was really encouraging for them and also for the Church. Sometimes things can go wrong but God still knows this and can bring encouragement through it.

Another time I got two words of rebuke for two different people at the same time. I didn't know what to do. So I phoned a wise old Christian friend of mine and asked for his advice. He asked me did I love the two people? If I did, then I could give the words. If not, then I shouldn't. After I'd spoken with him I thought about the two people. One of them I genuinely loved and knew the word was for him. The other person I realised I didn't love, and the word I thought I had was simply coming out of my frustration with him. It clearly wasn't from God. So I only gave the word to the person I loved. He acknowledged that what God had said was true and repented of the thing he was doing wrong. It was a real turnaround for him. It's always important that we check our motives when we give a prophetic word. Make love your goal.

Once I had a dream and in this dream I was in the porch of a friend's house. I apologised to him for something I had done to him which was wrong and then I woke up. My friend had moved house and I had never visited his new house. That week he was having a small group in it so I went along. At the end of the meeting I was leaving and standing in his porch. It was exactly as I'd seen in the dream. So I apologised for what I'd done to him and said I was sorry. That cleared the air between us and made things good again.

Notes of a Seer

I had a Christian friend of mine who was struggling with his faith. He had come to a place where he couldn't hear God anymore in any way. Because he knew I was someone who did hear from God he asked me to ask God, right there and then, for something he wanted to say to him. I told him that God wanted him to know that He loved him. I know God always wants to say that. But I didn't feel comfortable with what I'd done and asked God about it afterwards.

God told me that I wasn't my friend's intermediary. It wasn't my job to stand between my friend and God. That was Jesus' role. I was wrong to have given in to the pressure from my friend. I loved him and wanted to help him, which was good, but I should have told him I would wait on God later and see what He wanted to say. That was when God would have told me the reason why he wasn't hearing from Him. It was because of his relationship with Him and that he had wandered far from Him. I said I was sorry to God and asked Him to forgive me.

It's really important that we don't give in to pressure to prophesy over people there and then. That's especially hard if it's a really close friend. You love them and want to encourage them. But always wait on God first and tell them that's what you'll do. If God gives you something you can share it. But it's also fine if He doesn't.

Another time someone came to me when their life was a big mess. They posed this question to me: Since God is so awesome and amazing it must be possible for Him to speak one word that would be the key to sorting out a person's whole life and fixing any mess. Given that this was possible, he then asked me to ask God what that word was for him and to speak it to him now!

Of course I told them that's not how the prophetic works! But people can come to you with huge expectations and you need to be prepared to mostly disappoint them. Quite often the words that God gives you will not be the answer they were looking for. They might want to know about a job promotion, or a decision about moving to a different city, or a whole host of things they feel are hugely important. But God knows exactly what they need to hear. And we need to go with that. Don't be manipulated, bullied or persuaded to do anything other than speak what you hear God saying. And if He's saying nothing, you shouldn't either. And always, always remember: make love your goal.

Chapter 20: Am I going crazy?

When you talk about the unseen realm, it's easy for people to think that you're some flaky Christian who's making it all up. I was ministering at a Church once, and the guy who was leading the meeting asked me this question: "Is it true you've read the Bible as many years as you've been a Christian?" I told him that was true. He then said he wanted to tell the congregation this fact because he didn't want people thinking I was some sort of flaky Christian. I love this guy, and I love his heart. I know it's difficult sometimes for people to know where to put people who are having these spiritual experiences. But I'm grateful that he made room for me.

In writing this book there are two groups of people I'm hoping it will encourage and help. The first is those who are having similar kinds of experiences and don't know what to do with them. If that's you, then you need to know that you're not going crazy! God has a purpose for them. It's for your edification and also for the edification of the Church. Ask God for the wisdom to know what to do with them – be that prayer or sharing for encouragement.

The second group of people are those in leadership positions. Please make room for the seers. We love God, love His Church and love the lost. How God speaks to us might not be everyone's experience, but our goal is to see the Church built up, to see every part working together, and to see God glorified in all that we do. We know that's your goal too, so let's work together to the glory of God.

Chapter 21: Prayer of impartation

I've talked about impartation before and how important it is, so I wanted to add a prayer of impartation here. As you read this, imagine I'm standing in front of you and laying my hands on your head.

Dear Lord Jesus, I pray for the person reading this prayer right now. I pray that you would open their eyes to the unseen realm. I pray for an impartation of the Holy Spirit's power in their life. May they see things they've never seen before - Spiritual things. May they see angels. May they see demons cast out. I pray for them as they go to sleep – that you would speak to them in their dreams. And when they wake up, I pray that you would give them the interpretation of the things they have dreamt about. I pray that they would see visions, open visions, would experience trances. I pray that you would use them powerfully in the prophetic. That you would use them to reveal the secrets of people's hearts and they would see people saved. Whatever they know of you now, Lord, I pray that you would reveal more. Reveal more of yourself. Use them for your glory. I pray that love would always be their motive.

In the name of Jesus,

Amen!

Notes of a Seer

Appendix A: Armour Proclamations

The hour has come for me to wake up from my slumber because my salvation is nearer now than when I first believed. The night is nearly over, the day is almost here. So I put aside the deeds of darkness and put on the armour of light. I clothe myself with the Lord Jesus Christ and do not think about how to gratify the desire of the flesh. (see Rom 13:11-14)

The Blood of Jesus

• Through the blood of Jesus I am redeemed out of the hand of the Devil
• Through the blood of Jesus all my sins are forgiven
• Through the blood of Jesus I am continually being cleansed from all sin
• Through the blood of Jesus I am justified, made righteous, just-as-if-I'd never sinned
• Through the blood of Jesus I am sanctified, made holy, set apart to God
• Through the blood of Jesus I have boldness to enter into the presence of God
• The blood of Jesus cries out continually to God in heaven on my behalf

Give thanks to the Lord for He is good; His love endures forever. Let the redeemed of the Lord say this – those He redeemed from the hand of the foe. (Ps 107:1-2)

In Him I have redemption, through His blood, the forgiveness of sins, in accordance with the riches of God's grace that He lavished on me with all wisdom and understanding. (see Eph 1:7-8)

This is my prayer: that God may fill me with the knowledge of His will through all spiritual wisdom and understanding; that I may live a life worthy of the Lord and please Him in every way: bearing fruit in every good work, growing in the knowledge of God, being strengthened with all power according to His glorious might so that I may have great endurance and patience, and joyfully giving thanks to the Father, who has qualified me to share in the inheritance of the saints in the Kingdom of Light. For He has rescued me from the dominion of darkness and brought me into the Kingdom of the Son He loves, in whom I have redemption, through His blood, the forgiveness of sins. (see Col 1:9-14)

I walk in the light, as He is in the light, and the blood of Jesus, His Son, purifies me from all sin. (see 1 John 1:7)

Since I have now been justified by His blood, how much more shall I be saved from God's wrath through Him. (Rom 5:9)

And so Jesus also suffered outside the city gate to make the people holy through His own blood. (see Heb 13:12)

Since I have confidence to enter the most holy place by the blood of Jesus, by a new and living way opened for me through the curtain, that is, His body, and since I have a great priest over the house of God, I draw near to God with a sincere heart in full assurance of faith, having my heart sprinkled to cleanse me from a guilty conscience and having my body washed with pure water. (see Heb 10:19-22)

Therefore, since I am surrounded by such a great cloud of witnesses, I throw off everything that hinders and the sin that so easily entangles, and I run with perseverance the race marked out for me. I fix my eyes on Jesus., the author and perfecter of my faith, who for the joy set before Him endured the cross, scorning it's shame, and sat down at the right hand of the throne of God. I have come to Mount Zion, to the heavenly Jerusalem, the City of the living God. I have come to thousands upon thousands of angels in joyful assembly, to the Church of the firstborn, whose names are written in heaven. I have come to God, the judge of all men, to the spirits of righteous men made perfect, to Jesus the mediator of a new covenant, and to the sprinkled blood that speaks a better word than the blood of Abel. (see Heb 12:1-2, 22-24)

Helmet of Hope

But as for me, I shall always have hope; I will praise you more and more. My mouth will tell of your righteousness, of your salvation all day long, though I know not it's measure. I will come and proclaim your mighty acts, O Sovereign Lord; I will proclaim your righteousness, yours alone. Since my youth, O God, you have taught me, and to this day I declare your marvellous deeds. Even when I am old and grey, do not forsake me, O God, till I declare your power to the next generation, your might to all who are to come. (see Ps 71:14-18)

May the God of hope will me with all joy and peace as I trust in Him, so that I may overflow with hope by the power of the Holy Spirit. (see Rom 15:13)

I hold unswervingly to the hope I profess, for He who promised is faithful. (see Heb 10:23)

For everything that was written in the past was written to teach me, so that through endurance and the encouragement of the scriptures I might have hope. (see Rom 15:4)

Do you not know? Have you not heard? The Lord is the ever-lasting God, the Creator of the ends of the Earth. He will not grow tired or weary, and His understanding no-one can fathom. He gives strength to the weary and increases the power of the weak. Even youths grow tired and weary, and young men stumble and fall; but those who hope in the Lord will renew their strength. They will soar on wings like eagles; they will run and not grow weary, they will walk and not be faint. (see Isa 40:28-31)

This is my prayer: that the God of my Lord Jesus Christ, the Glorious Father, may give me the spirit of wisdom and revelation, so that I may know Him better; that the eyes of my heart may be enlightened in order that I may know the hope to which He has called, the riches of His glorious inheritance in the saints, and His incomparably great power for us who believe. That power is like the working of His mighty strength which He exerted in Christ when He raised Him for the dead and seated Him at His right hand in the heavenly realms, far above all rule and authority, power and dominion, and every title that can be given not only in the present age but also in the one to come, and God placed all things under His feet and appointed Him to be head over everything for the Church, which is His body, the fullness of Him who fills everything in every way. (see Eph 1:17-23)

Shoes of the Gospel of Peace

You will keep me in perfect peace because my mind is steadfast as I trust in you. (see Isa 26:3)
I have great peace because I love your law and nothing can make me stumble. (see Ps 119:165)

I am not anxious about anything, but in everything, by prayer and petition, with thanksgiving, I present my requests to God. And the peace of God, which transcends all understanding, will guard my heart and my mind in Christ Jesus. Finally, whatever is true, whatever is noble, whatever is lovely, whatever is admirable – if anything is excellent of praiseworthy – I think about such things. (see Phil 4:6-8)

I am not ashamed of the gospel, because it is the power of God for the salvation of everyone who believes: first for the Jew, then for the Gentile. (Rom 1:16 NIV)

Belt of Truth

Father, you are not a man, that you should lie, nor a son of man, that you should change your mind. You speak and then act. You promise and then fulfil. (see Num 23:19)

Jesus, you are the way, the truth and the life. No-one comes to the Father except through you (see John 14:6)

Holy Spirit, you are the spirit of truth. You will guide me into all truth. You do not speak on your own; you speak only what you hear, and will tell me what is yet to come. (see John 16:13)

Shield of Faith

I love you Lord God and I trust you. I love you Lord God and I trust you. I love you Lord God and I trust you.

Sword of the Spirit – the Word of God

The law of the Lord is perfect, reviving my soul. The statutes of the Lord are trustworthy, making me wise. The precepts of the Lord are right, giving joy to my heart. The commands of the Lord are radiant, giving light to my eyes. The fear of the Lord is pure, enduring forever. The ordinances of the Lord are sure and altogether righteous. They are more precious than gold, than much pure gold; they are sweeter than honey, than honey from the comb. By them I am warned. In keeping them there is great reward. (Ps 19:7-11 NIV)

I give attention to God's words; I incline my ear to what He says. I do not let them depart from my eyes; I keep them in the midst of my heart; for they are life to me and health to all my flesh. (see Pr 4:20-22)

Recommended Reading

There is More by Randy Clark

Angels on Assignment by Roland Buck

They Shall Expel Demons by Derek Prince

Listen to me, Satan by Carlos Anacondia

Free in Christ by Pablo Bottari

The Kiss of the Father by Julian C Adams

Whose word is it anyway? by Keith Hazell

The Panoramic Seer by James Maloney

The Dancing Hand of God by James Maloney

Chasing the Dragon by Jackie Pullinger

Face to Face by Anna Goodman

Developing Prophetic Culture by Phil Wilthew